5 Stages of Love

5 Stages of Love:

From Personal Development to Deeper
and Longer Lasting Relationships

WElationship 1

Yuri Bruce

WElationship Series:

Dedicated to all the couples and single people looking for a serious relationship.

Table of Content

Who Are We?

Hey Guys,

We are Yuri and Bruce! We are content creators. We got our start making how-to videos on Youtube. We talked about the fiance visa process and then the green card process (see more in our book *Fiance Visa to USA* for a breakdown of that process). As we helped people with their visas, they started asking us about our relationship. So we made videos about it. We talk about our success and failures and people seem to like it.

We decided to go a little deeper and write a book about it. And here it is.

This first book in our WElationship series is written from Bruce's perspective but all of the insights and experiences are from both of us.

Stay tuned for more books in the WElationship series!

Check us out on social media:

Youtube.com/yuribruceteam
Instagram.com/yuribruceteam
Facebook.com/yuribruceteam
Patreon.com/yuribruceteam
http://Yuribruce.com

1

Same Team, with the Same Dream

The text message read, "I cannot believe it's over"

"I really loved her"

"We were in a relationship for two years... what happened?"

People often talk to us about their relationships after seeing some of our WElationship videos online. Sometimes they ask for advice and sometimes it is just to talk to someone about their relationship.

This message came through on Facebook Messenger from our long-time subscriber whose fiancée had opted out of marriage and went back home to her parents. We were shocked because their relationship seemed solid. All we could do was listen, console him and tell him we had his back. Shortly after that, we got a message from another subscriber of ours who was getting a divorce after less than a year of marriage. This was another relationship that we thought would go well. After all, the guy was a doctor. She was attracted to him and seemed happy in the beginning to start a new life. But it turns out he was still involved with his ex, constantly arguing with her about money and flirting with random women online. Their relationship was over before it started.

It seemed like many couples we knew were having HUGE issues and all we could do was text them back as we enjoyed our second honeymoon in South Beach Miami after a three-day run through Disney World. We felt bad for our friends, but we were happier than we had ever been. We wondered why others were having such a hard time.

We thought to ourselves:
"Are we special?"
"Maybe we're just blessed"
"Maybe we met at just the right time?"

But after talking to 100s of couples we realize that there is one difference that stands out: WORK. We both work hard on the relationship.

What is special about our relationship is the work we each put into it and how we apply our effort. Beyond magic, beyond being "soulmates" and very attracted to each other, we put in the work every day.

We don't have all the answers and we have hard times. Despite what people might think, we do NOT have a perfect relationship. As much as we love each other, we each have our dramatic "Diva" moments, we have challenges, disagreements and very hard times that come out of nowhere. The continuous work on the relationship seems to be what's different between our relationship and the relationships of some of our unsuccessful friends. More importantly, how we put in that work for our relationship allows us to continue to fail forward and improve.

Having a relationship that feels like you are with a "soulmate" is something we realize that a lot of couples don't have. As much as I would love to call it destiny, fate ordained in the stars before we met, magical and divine I must admit that the real reason things are working so well is that we have applied our effort in the 5 stages explained in this book.

Every morning, there is a feeling of excitement of waking up next to someone we get to build our dreams and goals with. We get to explore life with someone we care about. We have each other's back all the time no matter what.

How does it feel? It feels like every day is your birthday and Christmas Day. The only drawback is that the ACTUAL Christmas Day does not feel as special anymore and your ACTUAL birthday is just another day. It feels like you are tackling life challenges as a team. And what happens is the visions and dreams of that team become bigger than any one member. It takes on a life of its own. With the level of effort applied in this simple formula, any willing couple can have this experience together. Comparing ourselves to others, we are typical. But the work that we put in not typical at all.

5 Stages of Love

When you make a commitment to a relationship, you invest your attention and energy in it more profoundly because you now experience ownership of that relationship.

- Barbara De Angelis

There are 5 Stages of Love:
1 - Self-Love
2 - Time Together
3 - Trust Building
4 - Team Support
5 - Dream Building

Also known as "STTTD" or just STD's for short! For love to succeed, you need STDs! Try to forget that one!

On a serious note, developing all 5 stages of love takes continuous work. What we noticed among some relationships is that they become too comfortable once they have their dream partner. They then stop working to please that partner and they stop working on their relationship. You cannot relax and act like you are single and living alone again. Partner inclusion remains a must throughout your relationship. No matter how good you think things are going to go with the person you are with, no matter how magical it feels, if you don't put in the work in all 5 stages of love, the relationship will not last:

After months of online dating, Bruce traveled halfway around the world to Cebu, Philippines, a tropical island paradise known as the "Queen City of the South" to find his soul mate. He found a love that he did not know he lost. He had the best time of his life with the woman of his dreams. He had never felt so connected to anyone. "Is this a spiritual connection?" he wondered. They became girlfriend and boyfriend. Then they broke up a few weeks later.

Tina met the most beautiful man she had ever seen in club PUMP. His name was Paul. He was a 6'2 Swedish Ragnarok Thor who could not dance, but WOW was he hot. He grabbed her hand and they disappeared into the crowded dance floor. The rest of the night was a hilarious, fun, pleasurable blur. The next morning Paul kissed her awake and proposed. Tina said no. They never saw each other again.

After 7 years of marriage, Joe and Lisa had two beautiful kids together, twins. Lisa's parents had not been supportive of her marriage to Joe because he was not Jewish, but they made it through that and many other challenges. They were great parents, went to parent-teacher conferences, became soccer parents and bought a minivan. They were the ideal couple, so it was a shock to everyone when they file for divorce.

Each of these relationships ended for the same reason, they did not work on all 5 stages... some did not even make it through any of the 5 stages.

Your Loving Magical, Soulmate, Dream Partner is Not enough

Even if you find your soulmate, meet your dream guy or girl, or fall in love with the father of your kids, or mother of your kids, if you don't put in the work on your relationship, it will not last.

You can have the most amazing sexual, emotional, spiritual attraction, experience, the most intensely passionate moments ever, but without both of you working hard for it continuously on all 5 stages, it will not work out.

Why? Why can't a soulmate be the answer? And what do we mean by "work"? Isn't a great relationship supposed to be effortless? What happened to "love is all you need"?

While it might be easy to love your partner, love is not enough for a long-lasting relationship. It does not make a relationship complete. Love is only one of the many parts that go into the story of a good relationship. Love is the stage, you must put your heart and soul into the performance.

When we say "developing all 5 stages of love take continuous work" we mean:

Self - Work on loving yourself so you can love others better.

Time - Spend time together. Start dating your partner and never stop.

Trust - Trust each other. Build and maintain trust with your partner.

Team - Support each other. Support the team.

Dream - Dream together.

STTTD! Or **sTd** for short.

Each stage is continuous. Evaluate where you are and keep improving. Look at all aspects of yourself and your relationship. Be honest about where you are with your relationship. Find room for improvements and improve. Work on the 5 stages with a holistic almost religious dedication. Be obsessed with improving them.

Is a great relationship effortless?
Whether you have a soulmate, an awesome parent to your kids or you have met the man or woman of your dreams, don't they deserve your very best effort?

If it is a great relationship, the more work you put in, the more you get out of it. Of course, if you are in a one-sided relationship your efforts won't work. We are talking about a relationship where both people want to work for the sake of the team.

When Bruce Met Yuri: Even Soulmates Have to Work

We met on a video chat. When we saw each other for the first time we could not stop smiling. The physical attraction was immediate and powerful. But both of us wanted more than just a "pretty face". Our skepticism started to dwindle once we realized we could talk for hours and still want more. The connection and compatibility were there. I found her honesty with herself refreshing. But she was a bit young. As a divorced father of two, I was looking for someone older. I was 37 and she was 22, but her maturity and wisdom were a shock. We had an on again off again long-distance relationship. Then we met in person.

I flew to her country, the Philippines. Meeting for the first time was a spiritual experience. Just going for a walk, the colors were somehow brighter. The palm trees with bright green, the sky bright blue against diamond sea. Clouds were rendered in amazing 3D Graphics. None of it looked real. The moment was surreal. There is no doubt that the attraction was overwhelming. And as we talked, we thought "maybe we are soulmates."

Despite this magical experience, we still broke up. We have been married for a while now and looking back on it, we know why.

Writer Richard Bach said, "If you love someone, set them free. If they come back they're yours; if they don't, they never were."

Understanding this after breaking up with someone you REALLY love takes work on the first stage of love, Self-Love.

3

Stage 1: Self-Love

"If you can learn to love yourself and all the flaws,
you can love other people so much better.
And that makes you so happy."

-Kristin Chenoweth

In western society, one of the highest ideals is to be selfless. Heroes are given the highest medals of honor for being selfless. Saviors and prophets are praised for thousands of years for teaching selflessness. Organizations are given a head nod for selflessly donating millions for a good cause.

But if you look closely most of the biggest, most selfless givers give from a place of great abundance. A firefighter running into a burning building has trained to gain an abundance of strength, dedication, and skill to do what they do. Organizations who can give thousands usually have millions in collective assets. Large international organizations that donate millions have 100s of millions or billions in collective assets and net worth. You might be wondering, "But what about Jesus! He gave selflessly?" Yes. True. But as the only begotten son of GOD, I would say that he has a certain level of abundance.

How can you care for anyone if you can't care for yourself? How can you love you when you don't love yourself? How can you shelter anyone when cannot shelter yourself? If you think you can get away with loving a child without loving and caring for yourself, you may be ignorant of how deep love can go.

Selfless Love of the Self Fulfilled, Saman Kunan

2018, in Thailand, 12 boys and their coach wandered into the Tham Luang caves after soccer practice. They had gotten deep just before a flash flood trapped them inside. After nearly 2 weeks, they were found alive but rescuing them would require a 6-mile dive from professional divers against powerful currents in muddy water. Few people can make a dive this difficult.

Saman Kunan in a bike race

An ex-Thai Navy SEAL, Saman Kunan, volunteered to go back into service to help with the rescue. Seeing pictures of Saman Kunan raising his arms in triumph as he completed a triathlon or smiling in the middle of one his many adventure races through Thailand tells how much this capable and confident man loved life.

Saman Kunan with his wife Valeepoan Kunan

How much more did he care for those kids if he was willing to risk his own amazing and happy life to save them. Saman Kunan died while delivering supplies to them. They all made it out of the cave alive because of people like him. True story.

Place the Mask on Yourself First

"In the unlikely event that the aircraft cabin loses pressure, oxygen compartments will automatically open in the panel above your seat. Reach up and pull the mask to your face. This action will start the flow of oxygen. Place the mask over both your mouth and nose and secure with the elastic band as your Flight Attendant is demonstrating.

If you are traveling with children, or are seated next to someone who needs assistance, place the mask on yourself first, then offer assistance. Continue using the mask until advised by a uniformed crew member to remove it."

During the aircraft safety announcement, have you ever wondered why you must place the oxygen mask on yourself before you put it on children?

The reason is if the aircraft cabin loses pressure or oxygen at 40,000 feet you have as little as 18 seconds of useful consciousness due to hypoxia, oxygen starvation. You may not even know you have hypoxia until you can no longer breathe and fall unconscious. If you pass out, you cannot help anyone. The child might not be able to reach the oxygen mask. You cannot help them if you cannot even help yourself. And in life, it is the same way. You could see the oxygen mask as physical, financial, emotional and mental stability.

In a relationship, people are relying on you to get your oxygen mask, so you can help them with theirs which they may not be able to reach.

It is important to take care of yourself first. If you cannot help yourself, you cannot help anyone else.

You must get yourself together to truly help anyone else. Of course, there are occasions where you can help an old lady across the street. Or help a kid with homework. Or maybe helping homeless veterans or give tithes. We are not necessarily talking about stuff like that. We are talking about a serious relationship, commitments like bringing a child into this world. Things like having a long-term relationship with that special someone. We are talking about being in a position to give someone a lifetime of assistance. We are talking about oxygen. You need to have your life together before you can be completely ready for a long-term relationship.

When Bruce Met Yuri: Baggage Break Up

After visiting Yuri in the Philippines, I was sure that she was the one. I wanted to take her somewhere she had never been, Thailand. It was only a four-hour flight from the Philippines. So, we would meet there then fly to Bangkok together.

It sounded good, but something was wrong. Yuri was in a bad mood. She was not talking. And when she did it was short annoyed conversations. They call it "tampo" in the Philippines. It is a dish served cold, with 2 cups of silent treatment and just a dash of passive-aggressive irritability.

I sat in the window seat and put on my seatbelt. Yuri sat in the aisle seat next to me. She stared ahead into nothingness.

"Are you ok?" I asked.

"Fine," she mumbled and snapped out of her dazed depression long enough to put on her seatbelt. I had seen her like this in Boracay. She would get in these long moments of tampo and not talk. Something was wrong. I was still a new relationship, so I didn't know if it was triggered by something I did or if this was just how she was.

Whatever it was, I was sure that if she would just talk, we could get through it. Normally, it just lasted for a few hours and she was back to normal. But when we got to the airport in Thailand all hell broke loose.

After getting through customs, I shot over to an ATM to withdraw some Baht. I had saved about $1200 dollars which was more than enough for our four-day trip. We would not make the mistake of staying in the most expensive hotels like we had done in the Philippines. The plan was to spend a little on a cheap hotel because we would not be hanging out there anyway. The bank account said $400 USD. This had to be a mistake. I thought maybe I'd been a victim of identity theft. I check two more times and started to sweat.

"What the..." my first impulse was to call the bank and ask them what was going on... But then I realized what had happened. A feeling of dread poured over me. I wanted to scream as I dialed. I called my ex-wife.

My ex-wife had accessed my bank account and drained it. After overhearing the conversation Yuri wanted to go home. She was a young lady and did not want this kind of drama.

"Why would she still have access to your account?!"

She started crying in the airport and panicking that I had not booked a hotel.

"Greg never did this," she said through tears.

"Who is Greg?" I said even as I realized. It was her ex. "You know, what? You should go back to Greg. I am going to change your ticket, so you can go back to the Philippines."

She seriously considered it for a moment as she sat in silence. The worst part about it is that she had a look of disgust when she glanced over at me. She would not look for more than 2 seconds.

Arms crossed, she said, "I'll stay".

When I could not convince her to catch a flight home, I told her I would look for a hotel.

"Why didn't you book a hotel?" She started to panic again.

"Getting a hotel is easy. Anyway, I thought you wanted to go back to the Philippines?"

"Look, it's just that… Normally, I am used to the hotel being booked. And what are we going to do with $400 dollars?"

"Oh, you mean, Greg books everything in advanced?" I said.

"Yes, "she replied.

After more argument, we decided to stay in Thailand together. We had both decided it would be the last time we would see each other. From my perspective, it was: "Greg, takes better pictures." Tampo, Tampo, Tampo. "Greg was so romantic." From Yuri's perspective, I might as well still be married. What I called an "adventure" and "spontaneous", she called "unprepared" and "unorganized". Nothing like Greg!

We found a hotel. During the taxi ride, our anger was only interrupted by moments of fascination with Bangkok. It was a quiet ride.

Looking back at it, we both had so much to work on to move past our relationships with our exes. Ties and attachment to the past still needed to be cut. We were both so messed up that it is amazing we made it through that. I think most people would not have.

Relationships are way harder to work on if you still have ties to an old relationship. We still had a lot of personal issues to work out, so it is very clear why we could not maintain stability in the beginning. Therefore, it is so important with self-love to work on your own situation before you can really give to another person.

The Case of the Lost Dudes

Fast forward six years. It is 2017, we have a home in Colorado. We are becoming influencers on social media. We have challenges, but we are getting through it. We tell about some of those challenges online. We share our story to help others.

We got a message from a guy that wanted to know if his girl would still love him if he was having trouble. He had seen our story online and want to find someone that would stick by him like Yuri did with me.

"What kind of troubles are you having?" Yuri asked.

"Well, I want to go to the Philippines too. Like Bruce. I found my soulmate there. I really love this girl, you know? But I can't afford a ticket yet," the lost dude said.

"But once we are together, we can have kids, get married... Be happy, you know?"

"It's actually not that expensive depending on where you are in the United States. Just take your time and save up," Yuri replied.

"But I have to spend money on fixing my car. I have been having some issues with that," he said.

"After you fix your car, save up." She said.

"I don't have a job to save up yet. It has been stressful, and I have some bad emotional issues. Do you think she will still love me?"

What we told the Lost Dude was that he should focus on his own life before flying to the Philippines. We said he should get his financial and emotional life together before going any further. His goal was to go visit his girlfriend in the Philippines, get engaged and then petition her for a fiancée visa. But one of the main thing you must do for this kind of visa is proving that you make enough money to sponsor the foreign fiancée. You must make at least above the poverty guideline.

We did not tell him anything we didn't have to do ourselves. When we met both of us we're rebounding from serious lessons in life from our exes. What both of us had discovered at that time was that we wanted someone willing to work as hard as we did in a relationship. We were both independent people. Even though we had baggage, we were both positioning ourselves to be in a better relationship than we had previously had. We both had income. We were taking care of ourselves. So, when we met one another we were not dependent. Instead, we became interdependent. That has made all the difference in the world. When you meet someone who is a self-starter, emotionally and financially stable, you don't have to coddle and baby them.

The first and most important work that all of us need to do is to work on ourselves. We must take responsibility for our success and failure and we must do it consistently. We must work on ourselves physically, financially and emotionally.

Take care of Yourself Physically
Work on maintaining your health. Exercise weekly if you can, get regular checkups and eat right. Don't neglect hygiene. This might seem obvious to some, but we are surprised at how many people don't take the time to take care of

themselves physically. Especially since most people want their partner to do the same.

Work on your own Finances
"Money isn't everything. But I'd like to see you live without it." - Silverchair, Tomorrow.

Financial stability is important in western civilization. It allows you to have independence and more freedom to do the things you want. This is valuable to you and your partner.

If you don't make enough money to support yourself, find creative ways to do it. Research how to make money doing something you love or something know how to do very well. If you cannot think of any creative ways to make income, and you don't want to take risks doing something you like or love, then do something you don't like. Go out and get a job. If that job does not make enough then get more than one job that you don't like. It doesn't matter whether it's something you are passionate about or not, a job is a job. The bottom line is you must make more money. Continue that job even if it sickens you because one day you are going to reach your goals. ALWAYS put money aside and save for yourself, just in case there is an emergency.

Work on your Emotional State

Working on emotions is sometimes the hardest and the most subjective part of self-love and self-care. It starts with taking responsibility for your own actions, thoughts, and words. Admitting that there is a problem is another big first step. There are important tools you will need like forgiving yourself and forgiving others. It is not easy. Allow yourself to fail often, fail frequently and fail forward. Don't give up on being better but realize that failure is the most important part of getting success. Don't allow your fear of failure stop you from taking action. Just know that fear without action will still give you fear, just without results. Zero action = Zero results. You might as well do the things you need to do with or without the fear. Jump while you are scared! The fear won't change until you challenge yourself to go beyond it.

The Science of Taking Action

Take action with or without fear. Whatever the results are will give you direction in life. Sometimes you must take action first to find the target. In the military, they have a term called "Fire for Effect". It is when you estimate approximately where the target is and shoot.

You use the impact, fire or burst from the bullet or munition to aim better on the next shot. You are firing to get the effect, so you can get closer to the intended target. Taking action is like firing for effect. You set a goal to get as close to where you think the target is as possible. You take action (fire). You adjust based on the results. This works well on self-development and many other aspects of life. Take action to love yourself. Take action to care for your physical body and financial situation.

Don't waste time blaming others for your life situations. Take responsibility for it so you can move on. If you make someone else the cause of all your problems, you are taking power out of your own hands to fix those problems. Don't worry about stuff you cannot control. Don't waste time complaining about stuff you cannot control. Spend more time working on what you can control. You can control looking in the mirror and loving yourself. Appreciate the good things you see in your own behavior. When you can learn to love yourself, it will make you a better lover. Spend time with yourself at least 30 minutes a day without catering to other people's needs. It sounds selfish but the happier you are the better you can serve others. Ask yourself often, what do I want to do for myself today, tomorrow, the weekend and the following months? Everyone needs time to recharge. That is the reason why people need the time to go on long vacations. They get so drained that they feel the need to be gone for long. Another aspect you must do is to respect yourself (respect your decisions), it will allow you to respect others. The more you care about yourself, the better your capacity to care for others.

To find the person of your dreams, become the person of their dreams

You must work on yourself first before you help anyone else. To find the person of your dreams, become the person of their dreams. If you don't have your life together, having a child or getting married does not fix this. Appreciating life is a choice. Life is not always happy, sometimes there are storms. But when you're in a good place emotionally, you can appreciate the rain and the breeze even in a storm and appreciate the beauty of snow in the winter.

Some people might say that working on yourself first is "selfish". They can call it whatever they want. The bottom line is that if you cannot care for yourself, how can you take care of anyone else. Maybe you can help them a few times, but how long before you have given them the last of what you had for even yourself? Will they be able to help you when you have given them everything? How can you take care of a partner, be there for a friend? How can you care for children? how can you do any of these things if you don't care for yourself?

Working on yourself first is not just for single people. Maybe you already have kids, maybe you already have a partner, maybe you're already married. If so, personal development is even MORE important. The more stable you are as a father, a husband, a lover, the more you can give. These people in your life deserve the best version of you. Become the best by taking action to improve.

You can help more people for longer and more effectively if you are fully taken care of. The best person to take care of you is you.

4

Stage 2: Time

Dating is about finding out who you are and who others are. If you show up in a masquerade outfit, neither is going to happen.

- Henry Cloud

Keep dating. Spend quality time together to develop the love you have for each other. Not just when meeting someone for the first time, but when you have been married for 20 years! Keep it fun. Come up with surprises. Keep exploring each other's interests.

For example, I don't like shopping... Ok, I hate it. When I am shopping with Yuri, I usually just want to get in, get what we need and get out. But sometimes I see shopping as a date. It's an opportunity to spend time with her. Sometimes there is even a comic book store nearby and we can check it out together. What I really enjoy is learning more about her Filipino culture. So, when she makes a traditional dish, or we go to a

Filipino restaurant, it is always a date I look forward to. And I have gotten her into Marvel and Sci-fi! She still cannot distinguish between Star Wars and Star Trek, but I really appreciate her effort. It took spending time together to figure each other out. It wasn't always like this.

When Bruce Met Yuri: An Alley in Bangkok
We weren't even halfway through day one of being in Bangkok and both of us wanted to leave. I thought Yuri should re-connect with her "romantic" & "organized" ex who she kept talking about. And Yuri was wondering why I still had an account with my ex-wife who had just taken more than half of my travel money. We figured, "ok, we're in Thailand. We might as well check the place out. But when we get back. It is over for sure." Neither of us had to say it.

For dinner, and our first restaurant in Bangkok, we went to a terrible, overpriced, outdoor restaurant where I forgot my wallet. Yuri gave me that, "ARE YOU KIDDING ME?!" face. I laughed and said, "don't worry. I'll just go back to the room and grab it. It's not that far away." As I walked back from the hotel to the restaurant with my wallet, I got suspicious stares from the waiters. I was thinking to myself, if every day and night is going to be like this, it is going to be a long trip.

We had to figure out what we could do on 14,000 Baht (which was about 460 USD back then) in Thailand for four days. It turns out that you can do a lot. We had dates walking around the city. We got lost and argued about directions every day. I suck at directions and refuse to ask anyone how to get anywhere. We caught a local boat tour of the Chao Phraya River to see the Grand Palace. Everywhere we went we were met with Thai citizens who were very helpful and kind. We would often get the "local price" because everyone thought Yuri was Thai. She would have to explain, "I am from the Philippines." Sometimes they would laugh and not believe it because she looked so Thai!

It was at the Buddhist temples in Ayutthaya, Thailand that Yuri stared at me and smiled. She said, "You know, you are so respectful and good in each culture and with every person."

I replied, "The people here are amazing... Just like the Philippines. I love it.

We shared a love and appreciation for the ways, traditions, and food from other cultures, especially Thailand. We got excited about learning new Thai word and how to say them correctly. It was something that she did not have in the past and it felt good. Yuri was holding me, hugging me and staring into my eyes smiling. The strong feeling of connection was back.

While I had an unexplainable love for her, I was still thinking she might still have feelings for Gary. Greg, Gilbert... Or whatever his name was. I had doubts until our last night when we were lost again and trying to take a shortcut through a dark alley in Bangkok. Walking in the opposite direction was a group of young Thai men. Light from the city shimmered against the silhouette of 3 men. My ghetto/Spidey senses were triggered. Where I am from we call it, "you about to get got".

"Maybe walking through a dark alley in Bangkok is not a good idea," I thought. I noticed 3 more guys in the cab of a truck on our right and a guy leaning on a wall shrouded in darkness on the left and one just entering the alley behind us whistling tunelessly into the night without a care in the world. We were surrounded. Yuri picked up on it too. I was assessing the situation as I kept my pace smooth and calm. Yuri followed my lead.

I found myself smiling. If I am going to go out, these guys are going to feel me. "Hold my backpack," I said. I was planning out who I was going to hit in the face first. Yuri took the backpack, threw it on her back and hiked up her long dress to start kicking.

This was yet another confirmation that Yuri was the one. For all the dramatic diva complaining she had done, she was ready to fight in that alley back to back with me. She did not back down. If she was panicking, I did not see it. She was the one. The guys in the alley got closer.

What Can you Give in a Date?
When it comes to dating, most people only think about what they can get out of it. However, as a stable person who feels that you have enough, you start to consider what you can give to others rather than just what you can take. Don't get me wrong, everyone thinks about getting something in the relationship but as you mature in dating experience, you realize that a great relationship is about give and take. If you're one of the rare people on the dating scene that thinks about

what they can give to a good partner, then you stand out. You are a catch, and someone is looking for you!

Don't Stop Dating

Dating should never stop. Whether you already have a girlfriend/boyfriend, fiancé or you've been married for years, dating is continuous. And as you're dating think about what you can give to your partner, get to know them, listen and explore each other.

Our Friends Ron and Betty

Ron and Betty have been married for 30 years. Ron and Betty still kiss each other every day. They are a cute older couple. Betty giggles like a schoolgirl when she sees Ron parading around in a speedo. She knows when they get home from the beach they are going to have some fun. Sometimes they go out for a drink of Chardonnay, get a little tipsy, go home and have a good time. They are in their 60s and still having the time of their lives together and it's all because they still date. They give each other surprises, compliments, show affection, but the MOST important thing they give is THEMSELVES. They give their time, their vulnerability, their strength, their patience and their love for each other.

Dating is Exploring
Dating is also about exploration. Exploring your partner's desires and needs by listening. It can be as simple as asking each other "how is your day?" Explore how they feel about their job, their friends, their family and their life. Give them your undivided attention and listen. If they are shy, initiate the conversation. Let them know it is ok because you want to know more. Give them your time. Just you two together sharing a special moment that is yours. Not for family, not for the kids, not for friends. Just you two. Dating is not just going somewhere special, it can be doing something special in the same old places.

Finding Someone Special by Dating
If you don't have a partner in your life at the moment, dating is about finding that special someone and then getting to know them better. Cast a wide net, be persistent and you will find someone. If you are using dating sites, use 3-4 dating sites with a detailed profile and interact as much as you can on each. If you are going out to clubs, interact as much as possible. Most importantly, have fun with each person you

meet. Smile and be approachable to all. Flirt make jokes, tease, laugh and be playful. Play around with people to figure out more about them. Don't get serious too fast. Remember no matter how great it seems you have to get to know them. You are both in a new territory.

When you're dating someone new there is always a good chance that this relationship won't be long-term, but I have found that one of the keys of dating is focusing on what you can give to the relationship. It will push you to find a relationship with someone willing to give as much as you will in a relationship. When we say "give" we are not talking about money. If you are broke and single, you should not be dating. You should be working on your life and getting more stable (if you are broke go back to Stage 1: Self-Love). Money is important. It is something you talk about with your partner once things get a lot more serious. But in the early stages of dating, it should not be your main issue. What requires your undivided attention is giving and receiving emotionally. What can you give emotionally to this new person and will this person be willing to give back? Are you two even compatible? Only time will tell so take your time.

How do you know when you can stop dating and become more serious? You never stop dating. Remember dating is exploring, having fun, pushing boundaries, going out together and spending quality time. From dating, you can build more trust. Building trust is not always fun, but a long-term relationship cannot live without it.

5

Stage 3: Trust

Building trust means opening yourself up to your partner. Building trust has been one of the hardest things we have done because over the years we had both learned not to trust anyone. We both grew up in a difficult childhood with parents who had complicated lives. We had seen domestic violence and lived in broken homes. We grew up to be in our own relationships that didn't work.

When Bruce Met Yuri: Discovery and Death While in Thailand

We were in a dark alley in Bangkok surrounded by 8 guys. I had handed the backpack off to Yuri to prepare for a fight. I knew I could not win but I could fight like hell to keep them busy so that Yuri could run. Hopefully, they only wanted money. If so, I would give up whatever had if that was even an option. I just wanted Yuri to make it back to the hotel. But Yuri was gripping her long dress to prepare for a fight. She had muscular legs like the Street Fighter character

Chun-Li, so god help the man that gets kicked in the balls with those Lyla Espadrille wedges. That guy would lose his ability to have children but at least he would be castrated by fashionable women's footwear. Glass half full, right?

Luckily (for them), there was no fight. There was no robbery. Instead, we passed the 8 guys without incident. We made it through the alley and started laughing.

"Whoa, I thought for sure those guys were going to attack us!" I said.

"Oh my god," Yuri said. "Feel my heart." Her heart was pounding like crazy. My hands were shaking. My eyes were wide, and I was hopped up on adrenaline.

"Wow. It looked like you were about to fight along with me," I said still feeling her heart.

"Hell yeah," she said. I would give her something extra special that night... in bed. If you know what I mean. Wink, wink. Sex. I would give her great sex. That's what I am saying if you didn't get the innuendo.

Once again, Yuri had confirmed that she was the right woman. Instead of panicking, she got ready for action. We'd had a long day going all around Ayutthaya tourist attractions, visiting temples and seeing the history of Siam still standing proudly in stone. It was a day of quiet enlightenment as we kept the customs of taking shoes off in the temples and lighting candles in front of statues of Buddha. We laughed. We smiled. We ate great Thai food and learned more Thai with anyone willing to teach us.

The next day was different. Yuri was down. She was distant. And I would catch her staring off into nothingness again and again.

"Are you ok?" I asked. Her response was barely a nod.

Something was seriously wrong today.

"Are you upset because we have to leave later today?" I asked.

"No."

We sat in silence at breakfast. I had my usual Thai version of "American breakfast". Yuri sat staring into a cup of bitter black coffee. She was physically on the other side of the table but mentally elsewhere.

After breakfast, we sat outside on the steps of the hotel with no plans for the day.

"My mom just died," Yuri said.

"What?" I heard her. "Like, just now. Today? How?"

The tears finally came, and Yuri told me everything.

She explained that she and her sisters had been caring for their mom after her diabetes had got worse. She told me that her mom had been a troubled and bitter woman who had been tasked with caring for 8 other siblings. She had put a lot of pressure on her daughters. Especially if they had money. They loved their mom, but she was so hard to live with. Yuri talked about how it was growing up. All her difficulties with family.

Knowing more about her life and the level of pressure she had been under after meeting me, a "rich foreigner", explained a lot of other things. She would have bouts of depression, fits of anger, random tampo in the months that we had been together. That whole time she was going through issues with her family but would not tell me because she knew our relationship had potential. She did not want her personal family issues to get in the way of that.

Once she opened to trust me, we decided to go for a long walk to talk about everything. Before we knew it, we were lost again in Bangkok. Thanks to me, we had been lost every day but today we had to get back to catch a flight.

Starting to Build Trust

It takes a lot of quality time together to build up the trust you need for a long-term relationship. It is earned over time. And the amount of time it takes depends on both people in the relationship, so no one can tell you "It will take you exactly 1 year to build the perfect trust of 7.9!".

No one wants to trust because trust is risky business. You can think you have built trust for years and find out it only one-sided. The truth is that not everyone deserves your trust. You don't ever really know what a person is doing, who they are talking to, what their true intentions are with you. The best we can do is trust their judgment and take a risk.

Building Trust is a continuous process. Trust must be maintained throughout the relationship. Trust is hard to earn but easy to lose.

How Tony Gained and Lost Laura's Trust

We know a couple, Laura and Tony, who have been together for over 10 years. They have three kids. They've lived in two different countries together. And created a comfortable middle-class American life together.

Tony met Laura in South Korea. Laura was a Filipino citizen working in South Korea as a waitress and Tony was in the US Navy stationed at a Republic of Korea (ROK) Naval Academy in Chinhae.

Tony was not looking for a relationship... until he saw her. She wasn't just cute, she was very kind, courteous and there was just something about her that was different. He was a single, 6'2, Italian guy who did nothing but workout in his spare time, so other ladies in the restobar would flirt with Tony and try to get his attention. He only came for two things: soju and Laura. And the soju wasn't even good. He would usually keep ordering soju until Laura delivered it. And when she came he would talk to her.

She brought the fifth drink he ordered. "Here's your drink, sir."

"Thanks, Laura. How is your night going?" He said.

"It's going. 3 more hours left," she said looking at her watch.

"You should come and have a drink with me after work." He said.

"Why do you have so many drinks?" She pointed at the 5 shot glasses on the small table.

"I am waiting for you to drink with me," he smiled.

He would come to the same restobar and sit in the same seat just to flirt with Laura. It got to a point where the other waitress would tell him, "Laura is not here" if she was off that night and he just would leave.

Laura was used to American military guys flirting. She was not into them because usually, they were only after one thing. And they were usually married. But with persistence and a winning smile, Tony eventually got her on some dates.

They found that they really liked each other's company. It was fun to hang out with Tony.

"Actually, the main reason I did not go out with you at first is that I thought you were an alcoholic," she told him.

He admitted that he only ordered that many so that she could come to him.

"Why didn't you just ask me? You didn't have to order the drinks. But the tips were a nice touch."

Over the course of a couple of years in Korea, they developed a relationship. He proposed to her at her job. Some of those other girls were very jealous.

They got married and Tony used the spousal visa process which took them 1 year to complete and cost about $2000 dollars with all the fees that go into the visa process.

They lived on base together in South Korea. At the end of his tour, they had to move to another base in Norfolk, Virginia. They settled down and bought a home. They had three kids. Laura was a stay at home mom. She dedicated herself to the family. Everything seemed fine until Tony started being a little bit more distant. She wonders why. They weren't spending time together. They were barely talking anymore.

Tony volunteered to go back to Korea. It would be a short tour without his family. He left, and they still were not talking much. The kids were out of school but doing ok during summer.

After a few months of being apart, Tony sent her an email. The email was meant for someone named, Seo-Yun. It was an affectionate message to Seo-Yun talking about their next trip to Jeju Island. They had apparently been seeing each other the entire time he was in Korea. Laura was devastated.

She confronted him about it and he had to make a decision.

He didn't want to abandon his kids so at the end of his tour in Korea he went back to Virginia. He tried to fix things, but it was unclear if that would ever happen. The three-month fling he'd had in Korea had jeopardized the 10 years of trust they'd build together. The family they built was broken. They stayed together for the sake of the kids, but they were just not close anymore. Essentially, they were just roommates co-parenting their kids. The kids could see that they were distant from one another. Trust has to be built and maintain.

Knowing When to Trust

Before you take this leap, you need to be sure this person and their ACTIONS are worth the risk. What can they do right now in your life that is worth the risk of a broken heart? And what can you give them to make it worth their risk?

One sign of trust is when someone tells you something that is hard for them to say. Something that does not make them look good, but it is the truth. Most people tell stories to make them look good even if they messed up. But if they say something that is personal and that they have not told many people, then that is a sign of real trust. They trust you with information that can hurt them. Never betray that trust. Once you feel compelled to tell this person something personal, something you have not told many people, something that makes you vulnerable then you know you trust them. Not many relationships make it to this stage. And even less make it through this stage and keep maintaining the trust because it can be hard. Sometimes the trust is built up and lost because somebody in the relationship cheats or stops telling the truth. It is hard to recover unless you have already graduated from this stage and moved to the next. The next stage is supporting each other and becoming a team.

6

Stage 4: Team

"Alone we can do so little; together we can do so much."

– Helen Keller

"Teamwork begins by building trust. And the only way to do that is to overcome our need for invulnerability."

– Patrick Lencioni

As hard as trust is to get and maintain, it is just the beginning. Long-term relationships take more than just dating and trust. You must work to support each other. Supporting your partner and accepting your partner's support is a level beyond trust. You are becoming interdependent.

Interdependent vs. Dependent

There is a big difference between being dependent on your partner and being interdependent. Dependent means you rely on your partner to support you and you bring nothing or very little to the relationship. You are a dead weight that your partner carries. Interdependent means you both carry the full burden of the relationship and each of you brings a lot to the team.

I can give you an example, you and your partner are traveling on the freeway in a car and it breaks down. You have to get the car to the side of the road. If your partner is completely dependent on you, they will sit in the passenger's seat and do nothing while you get out and push and steer the car to safety. If they are nice but completely dependent on you maybe they will get out of the car and watch you push. Or maybe they are not so nice and completely dependent on you, so they scream from the passenger's seat, "can't you go any faster? Your steering the car too far left!"

If you and your partner are interdependent and the car breaks down on the freeway you both get out of the car and push it to safety. Or maybe one of you steers while the other pushes the car. But you both take action to get the car to safety then you both work to fix the car and you're back on the road.

The more you work on yourself and your relationship, the more you realize your own strengths and weaknesses. You notice what you're good at, what you are bad at and what your partner is good at and what they are bad at. Working toward supporting each other means complimenting each other's strengths and weakness. It is amazing what you can do as a supportive team. But it is toxic to be with someone who you cannot trust and who is not supportive.

The Final Story of Tony and Laura

Tony and Laura were now in a 10-year relationship that they no longer wanted. They stayed together for the sake of their kids. Tony had gotten bored with the relationship, so he would often go online and flirt with women from all over the world. Laura's anger had turned into disgust. They did not sleep in the same room. When Laura did give in and have sex with him, she felt shame and Tony felt pity. They spent as much time away from each other as possible. They put on a good show when neighbors came over, but after a while, they did not care who knew. Every day it was harder to live this lie. Laura did not care what Tony did and Tony did not care what Laura did. Tony continued to go to work and come home. Laura continued to cook, clean and take care of the kids.

When Laura started looking very sick, Tony noticed but he did not react. Was it that he did not care? Or maybe he just didn't really think that it was serious.

Here is a list of thing Tony did not say:

"You are not looking good. Go to the hospital now."
"You have lost a lot of weight suddenly. Are you ok?"
"You look frail, pale and sickly. Do you need to get a checkup?

Maybe he knew that if he said anything that she would not listen. Laura was a 135-pound woman that had suddenly drop to 95 pounds. She was weak and pale. Something was very wrong. But instead of going to the doctor, she bragged about her new diet.

But it was not the diet making her lose this much body mass. It was cancer. It seemed very sudden when she passed away. But it was not sudden.

There had been something wrong for almost a year. Would things have been different if she had gone to the doctor? No one knows.

This is based on a true story. I really don't want to talk about this story. It gives me no pleasure to think about it. She is survived by her friends, family, and children. What we keep asking ourselves is: Why didn't Tony make her go to the hospital? Did they not care or support each other enough to even do that? More importantly, why didn't she care for herself enough to go to the hospital?

The tragedy framing this young woman's death is that even if it meant caring for the kids and even in the face of death Laura and Tony did not seem to rely on or trust each other. In the end, their lack of trust in the relationship was just as cancerous as the disease that took her.

Working on yourself, dating, learning to trust and support each other is not just about avoiding the inconvenience of being with an incompatible person, this is about your life.

I Blame Laura

This may sound cold, but I blame Laura. Yes, Tony cheated and broke trust. Maybe they did not develop enough trust to develop teamwork? I don't know. But the very first stage of love is Self-Love. And that means working to take care of yourself. She did not care enough for her own physical well-being to go get checked out by a doctor. She must have suspected something was wrong at some point. Cancer usually takes a while. Maybe the doctors would not have been able to do anything, maybe they could have only slowed it down, but the thing is we will never know because she never went to the doctor to find out. Taking care of your physical self is just as important as taking care of your mental, emotional self. For the sake of everyone who loves and depends on you, WORK ON YOURSELF FIRST!

Life is Too Short to Be with Someone That Does Not Support You

We have made a compelling case that Tony and Laura did not support each other. They did not make it to that stage. Or maybe only one of them had trust and support. But one is not enough for a team. I think it is sad because life is already hard enough without having to live with someone you don't like. Why would you want to waste a minute of your precious life with someone you are not willing to support or who is not willing to support you? Why would you want to be with someone who won't help you push the car when it's broken down? And who would want to give a piggyback ride to someone stabbing them in the back?

You need someone you trust enough to show your weakness too. We all have flaws. We all make mistakes. That is what being human is all about, failing often and failing forward. That means getting better when you get back up. The keyphrase is GET BACK UP. Get on your feet and keep going. Life on Earth is not for the quitters. Trust in your partner's strengths and if they can trust in your strengths you can have the interdependence of a solid team. I cannot promise you there won't be storms ahead, but if you have a teammate to weather it with it makes you motivated enough to kick that storm's ASS!

Interdependence only works if you have worked on yourself, gotten to know and like each other by spending time together and learned to trust each other. If the people in the team are not developed enough, if the relationship has not matured over time to develop trust, then that house of cards will be blown away with the first gust of wind. Hell, someone can just come by and blow it down! If a couple has is not dating, how can they get to a point where they gain deeper trust? And how can you depend on someone you don't trust? All the stages of love are related.

When Bruce Met Yuri: Every Hero Has a Kryptonite

Only now that I am older, wiser and able to swallow my pride and say that it was me. I am the one that got us lost every day that they were in Thailand. EVERYDAY. Including our last day when we had an international flight in a few hours. Now we really needed to get back to the hotel, get pack our stuff and call a taxi. But I was leading us deeper and deeper into the guts of Bangkok. From the economic lungs of downtown with its billion-dollar skyscrapers breathing life in the financial system of Thailand down deeper into the seedy back alley where the ladyboys look better than the hottest Thai girls. Gender is bent and any cultural reality that you cling to is relative. And I know what you are thinking right now, "Bruce, why are you bringing up beautiful Thai ladyboys and this book is supposed to be about 5 stages of love." And I will answer you and say until you have seen a Thai ladyboy you will never understand so shut up. The point is, we were lost and on the brink of madness.

Once again, the city has swallowed us up and we were on 8 Soi Sukhumvit 27 by Radisson Blu but I am so bad with directions that it might as well have been Kansas.

We were lost until I humbly accepted Yuri's suggestions. Or actually, it was more like Yuri snatched the map out of his hands and started walking. For whatever reason, Google maps and GPS was not working. Connectivity was not reliable at all. It was in and out depending on what part of Thailand we were in. So, we had resorted to grabbing one of those free maps from the hotel we were in. Thank goodness it was in English.

You would think with both my Army and Air Force training, I would be able to figure out a map. Yuri had hair clinging to her sweaty brow and she kept complaining about her feet. She had INSISTED on wearing wedges.

This vacation together was very informative. I had learned that the wild native diva, outside of her natural habitat, does not walk unless there are red carpets on her path and roses thrown at her feet. She might be a diva, but I had to admit she really knew how to navigate the maze of Bangkok. I got over my injured pride and just relied on her bird brain instinct for direction.

"I feel like I have been here before." She said as she walked quickly ahead only glancing at the map.

We got back to the hotel just in time to grab our luggage, catch a cab and make our flight back to Cebu, Philippines.

Beyond Pride is Interdependence
We did not realize how much pride we each had until we met each other. We both grew up taking care of ourselves and making a way out of no way. I started working at 8 and kept finding jobs like mowing lawns, paperboy, library book shelver until I joined the military, learned a trade to have a career. Yuri left her home in Cebu at age 15 to work in Manila as a home helper,

worked to put herself through college to do work as a virtual assistant. We had learned to rely on people as little as possible. We learned that if we want to survive, we must work. If we want something, we had to work for it. Nobody is obligated to give you anything, so you better get your own.

So, when I met someone as driven and hardworking as I was, I was impressed. Maybe even a little intimidated. It took time to accept someone else's help on directions in a foreign city let alone assistance in LIFE.

Once you have a team, you can dream together.

7

Stage 5: Dream

"Teamwork makes the dream work."

-Bang Gae

If you trust your partner and support each other you are officially a team. You don't need our congratulations because being a team is its own reward! If you don't feel like you are a team with your significant other, then let me tell you being a team is awesome. If you WANT to be a team implement the work in this book.

The Power of WE
Being a team is very powerful. Both of you are committed because you both realize the relationship is something much bigger than you. And you both learned to be interdependent on one another. For us, it has created a synergy that works way beyond anything we could have imagined. We have been able to manifest big dreams together.

We had traveled all over the Philippines, partied in Thailand three times and visited Hong Kong.

All that was fun, but we could only meet every few months. After two years of long distance relationship, we'd had enough of being apart (see *WElationship 2 on long distance relationships*). Yuri came to the US on a visa and we got married (see our book, *Fiancé Visa to USA!* for more on the K-1 visa process). This was one of the first big dreams that we turned into a goal and then accomplished together.

Once we were finally living together it was a new life for us. And we were starting from scratch. In the divorce, I had lost my house and half of my income to maintenance support and Yuri was starting a new life in a new country.

We were in a small one-bedroom apartment with no furniture, no plates, bowls or utensils. The first night all we had was an air mattress and a few boxes of our clothes and books. We used the boxes as a kitchen table. It sounds sad, but it was amazing because we had each other. We were no longer in a long-distance relationship. We had candlelit dinners on our kitchen box and we supported each other. We knew things would get better because we would make it better. I supported Yuri as she started her immigration process and helped her to adjust to American life. Yuri supported me as I started a new job.

We started to make plans on how to get out of this financial rut. We thought about where we wanted to be in 5 years and how we could get there. We wrote our dreams down and gave ourselves a time of completion. The dreams were officially goals put into action!

Some of our goals included:

- Buy property and get into real estate
- Create a profitable business
- Get rid of debt and fix our credit
- Move into a better place

We had a few challenges on the horizon. The debt was causing a lot of stress and my kids were living with us more and more in the one-bedroom apartment. It was way too small for a family of four.

So, I worked at two high level IT jobs for one year. It was brutal. I was always tired from staying up late to get work done and rarely had time off because of all the overlap of both jobs. But the significant extra income allowed us to pay off a large portion of the debt and save over 10K.

Paying off so much debt increased our credit score and allowed us access to over 40K in available credit which we used responsibly. Since the kids were now living with us full time, we were able to make a deal and move into my old house. I gave up my extra job. Once she got her green card and her driver's license, Yuri was able to get a job to bring in more income.

With the 10k we decided to aggressively learn more about business and stocks. Within 2 years we had obtained most of the main goals we had written down.

We made a lot of mistakes, lost money, fell and got up again. By the 3rd and 4th year we had the financial maturity and disposable income to buy real estate and create small assets.

It was all a dream. We turned that dream into a goal by writing it down and taking action. We had enough stability in our relationship to be able to take risks, fall and get back up.

We have been surprised by the power of being a team. We can accomplish way more together than we could have done apart because we have each other's back. And you know, we even support each other's individual goals which are equally important.

Anyone can do what we have done. Neither of us was a child prodigy. We have been more like outcasts who were teased for being weird or sidelined for looking different. We don't have the looks that society deems as "model material". Any talents that we have are mostly overlooked. The only thing special about us is that we are action takers who would rather work on goals than talk about dreams.

Dreaming together is not about just business and money. One of our goals is to travel to Bali. We had a goal of spending more time with the kids. You could have a dream of losing weight, gaining muscle, talking more, becoming a painter, running a marathon whatever, it is, you should share it with your team, so they can support you, motivate and push you. Or maybe even join you!

Even if the goal is for only one of you, how awesome is it to get support or be a part of their goal? The point is to take action on a dream together. Share the dream. Write it down. Turn it into an actionable goal with tasks and a timeline.

8

Keep Working On it

We have addressed all 5 Stages of Love:

Stage 1 - Self-Love. Love yourself first. Care for yourself financially, physically and emotionally.

Stage 2 - Time. Spend quality time together. Date or find a date and put in the time.

Stage 3 - Trust. Build and earn trust in your relationship. Both must learn to trust.

Stage 4 - Team. Build a team by supporting each other and being interdependent.

Stage 5 - Dream. Create and share dreams together. Make them into goals and take action.

Keep working on all these steps continuously. Evaluate where you are on each step and take action to make improvements.

Each step is very important if you want to keep the relationship going strong. Understand that it is not enough to find a soulmate and live happily ever after. There is no happily ever after. First, who the hell is happy all the time? Life is a full spectrum of emotional peaks and valleys with a complete landscape of obstacle courses.

You need someone who is ready to take that adventure through all four seasons of life. Somebody willing to help you push that car when it breaks down. The keyword is "WHEN" it breaks down because it is only a matter of time.

The point is that it takes work to develop a relationship over time. You nurture that relationship with trust and love you build for one another continuously.

Made in the USA
Coppell, TX
19 April 2025

48443739R10052